STEP AWAY
from
THE DRILL

*Change The Way You Lead
Your Dental Business For More
Control, Fun and Profit*

LAURA HATCH, M.S., FAADOM

Step Away from the Drill
Published by Dental Rock Star Publishing
Copyright © 2017 by Laura Hatch, M.S., FAADOM

All rights reserved.

Dental Rock Star Publishing
10755 Scripps Poway Parkway Suite 413
San Diego CA 92131
Email: dentalrockstarpublishing@gmail.com

Limit of Liability/Disclaimer of Warranty:

Publishing and editorial team:
Author Bridge Media, www.AuthorBridgeMedia.com
Project Manager and Editorial Director: Helen Chang
Editor: Katherine MacKenett
Publishing Manager: Laurie Aranda
Publishing Assistant: Iris Sasing

Library of Congress Control Number: 2017950483

ISBN: 978-0-9988496-0-7 -- softcover
978-0-9988496-1-4 -- hardcover
978-0-9988496-2-1 -- ebook

Ordering Information:

Quantity sales. Special discounts are available on quantity purchases by corporations, associations, and others. For details, contact the publisher at the address above.

Printed in the United States of America

*"It's not just about your dentist's capability and skill.
It's about people: relating to our patients as people first,
offering them great service, and promoting their health."*
— Laura Hatch

As a special thank you for purchasing *Step Away from the Drill* and your commitment to take your leadership and practice to new heights, please visit www.frontofficerocks.com/Iboughtthebook to access your free *Step Away from the Drill* official study guide. The study guide is designed to support you while you navigate each of these chapters. In it, you will find key questions to ask yourself and your staff, actionable steps to take right now in your office, and downloadable resources such as sample documents, policies, and free videos from my proven training program.

CONTENTS

ACKNOWLEDGMENTS

Before Front Office Rocks became a reality, I was the office manager in my husband Tony's dental practice. He saw in me the ability to partner with him and to build something from scratch together. When ideas about a video training program began buzzing around my head, Tony was there, supporting me, listening to me, and pushing me to push myself and start this company. I want to thank Tony for his love and unending support of my dreams, my ideas, and my crazy schedule. He is so much more than a business partner; he is my partner for life. Thank you for recruiting me and introducing me to the world of dentistry.

I want to thank my children, Nick and Alex, for their unconditional support and love of me and my dream of writing this book and starting Front Office Rocks. They are always willing to jump in and help in any way they can—even as actors in my videos. I love you both, and I would not be where I am today without you.

I also want to thank my rock star team at Front Office Rocks.

First, I want to thank Mark and Janelle for believing in

me when this was just a dream, and for always pushing me to be the best version of myself. If it were not for you two, Front Office Rocks would still be stuck as a small business with a bad logo.

Next, to my entire team, our dynamic works, but it works because we work at it. Each of you puts effort into the success we realize each day. We keep in touch, we share a group calendar, we know when each other's children are sick or when we have family commitments. Instead of shaking our heads and wondering how it will all get done, we just do it. We do it for our clients and for each other. This group of people scattered among three time zones and five states sets objectives and goals and uses the tools at its disposal to stay on track. Thank you, Mark, Janelle, Priscilla, Nicole, Christina, Missy, and Racquel for your commitment to our team.

Lastly, I would like to thank Paul and Joshua for being the dentists whom I tested this book with, and Shivi for always being supportive of me with both our dental office and my business. And I want to thank all my dental office staff members, current and past. If it were not for you guys, I would not have the amazing experiences to draw from to share in this book.

FOREWORD

Part of what attracted me to dentistry was the diversity of the day-to-day business. Dentistry is a business of art. It is a business of science. Above all, though, it is a business of relationships. Those relationships are wide and far reaching.

The relationship with the patient, the relationship with the team member, the relationship with the specialist or referring dentist—all of these must be fostered and constantly nurtured in order to thrive.

Think about all the headaches that come up during your day at the practice. Now think about how developing better communication skills could help remedy these issues.

Let's start with something we have all experienced and which happens all too often: a crown that doesn't fit and needs to be remade. Remakes are expensive because of the time involved in producing them. Maybe that crown didn't fit because the provisional came out and the patient did not return to have it recemented. Had we communicated the importance of the provisional to the patient, he or she would have returned right away to get it recemented and the crown would fit.

Or maybe the crown didn't fit because the assistant left the interproximal contacts open, and the adjacent teeth moved while the final crown was at the lab. Had we communicated the importance of good, solid contacts on the provisional to the dental assistant, a better provisional would have been made and the crown would fit.

Perhaps the laboratory fabricates all their crowns to be too light on their interproximal contacts and occlusion by design to reduce remakes from less meticulous dentists. Had we communicated with the dental lab what our expectations were in our restorations, the crown would have been made better and would fit.

Or maybe the patient was scheduled three months later to have the crown delivered. The longer the patient wears a provisional, the bigger the chance the final restoration won't fit. Had we communicated better with the scheduler about the importance of a timely seat appointment, the crown would fit.

This is just one example of how better communication can impact our profitability and sanity. You might be thinking, "I have a CEREC, so all that stuff about a provisional is garbage!" In that case, you would be right. However, the need for timely and thorough communication applies to nearly every problem we face on a daily basis. So all you CEREC users still need this book!

Laura Hatch has her thumb on the pulse of communication within the dental office. Better communication within our practices sets us up for success. This book will give you the tools you need to communicate better. Starting with the team, Laura shows us how to better communicate our expectations to every position within our office. From big-picture ideas like determining why we come in to the office every day, all the way to the fine details of how patient hand offs should be executed, this book offers complete solutions for enhancing your practice's performance.

By increasing and improving our communication, we become better leaders and better dentists, thanks to Laura Hatch!

—Joshua Austin, DDS MAGD
Private Practice
Managing Editor,
Dental Economics "Pearls for Your Practice"
and Product Navigator E-Newsletter

INTRODUCTION

Sleepless Nights

You are a dentist.

You probably got into dentistry because you wanted to help patients live a longer, healthier life. You may have chosen this profession because you liked the tools, handpieces, and fun gadgets in the lab. And yes, at some point, you more than likely chose dentistry to make money.

In dental school, you learned how to diagnose and treat cavities or gum disease. Then, after years of clinical training, they sent you into the world, saying, "Good luck. You are now a dentist. You're on your own! Go open a business and help patients." That is likely when the sleepless nights started.

Are those sleepless nights caused by the stress of crown margins or helping patients with gum disease? No. What keeps you up at night is the business side of things. *Is the patient going to show up for the appointment? Do my staff members know how to schedule appropriately? Will they collect the money my patients owe?*

And now here you are, picking up this book. You don't

know what to expect from your front office team, you are tired of not knowing what your employees do up there, and you want to see growth. Do you know how to hold your team accountable? You may ask your employees to fill your schedule or to collect money, and then go into your office and cross your fingers, hoping it happens.

That insecurity and lack of control means that *you* are working for *them*.

Many dentists don't go on vacations because they can't afford to take the time off. Some pay the bills each month but, in the end, are unable to put money toward retirement or pay for their children's education. But the staff gets paid. The lab bills get paid. The dental supply companies get paid.

The only person really suffering on Friday night or at the end of the month, trying to pay the bills, is you.

There must be a better way.

Change Your Hat

There is a way out, and it involves changing your hat.

In dental offices, as in most small businesses, everyone on the team wears different hats, which represent the different roles we play. Dentists are trained to wear their dental hats. You need to wear this hat when you diagnose, plan treatments, and perform dentistry. But you're not going to fix the failing business by doing root canals faster or learning how to place implants.

To fix your practice, you have to take off your dental hat, step away from the drill, and put on your business hat.

Even if you've never been trained in business, you need to understand what's going on in *your* business. You should learn the "why" behind what you expect your team members to do and how to make sure they're doing it.

You need to get in there and run the business like a CEO would run it—not like a dentist.

Your goal as a dentist is to help patients, but this is also your business. If you are not making any money, you won't be able to help anybody for very long. When you take on the responsibility of learning the business side, you control your destiny. You learn how a small business runs, how to grow the practice, and how to increase profit. Suddenly you become a better leader. You become more confident. Your stress level goes down.

Now, you sleep through the night. You don't worry if your patient is going to show up on Monday morning. You have more fun at work. You aren't afraid to talk to your staff members about what you expect from them.

What has changed between that sleepless Friday night to this happy Monday morning? It has nothing to do with dentistry, but everything to do with how you run your business. This is *your* business. Your degree is on the wall, and that is your name over the door.

You are in control.

Why Me?

Why should you listen to me? I'm not a dentist. I didn't go to dental school.

But I am married to a dentist.

In 2003, when my husband decided to open a scratch practice in Baltimore, Maryland, he asked me to quit my job and be his office manager. I knew nothing about dentistry, but I knew business. We opened a scratch practice with the right systems, policies, customer service, and team in place and grew from $0 to more than $1.4 million in under four years.

In 2007, we moved to San Diego and opened another scratch practice. We decided to move because of the amazing weather, but we really should have done our homework. We did not realize how much competition there would be in Southern California. Poor timing led to opening while the economy was down. To top it off, we were only twenty minutes from the Mexico border. In Maryland, patients don't say, "I need an implant; I'm going to Mexico."

But we knew that if we applied our knowledge—maintaining exceptional customer service, taking care of patients, getting them to accept dentistry, hiring the right staff members, training them well, putting in great systems—we could duplicate our first practice. And we did. We grew from nothing, again, and now have a thriving fee-for-service office that collects more than $250,000 per month and attracts on average fifty new patients a month.

Before long, other dentists started asking us what we were doing.

After talking to so many dentists, I realized what we were doing wasn't complicated, but it also wasn't taught in dental school. That is why I started speaking and training in the dental industry in 2007. I am a regular contributor in *Dental Products Report, Dentaltown, Progressive Dentist Magazine,* and many other dentistry publications. I am a featured interview on Dentaltown's podcast and in 2016 was named one of the Top 25 Women in Dentistry by *Dental Products Report.*

And I have the experience, knowledge, and resources to help you reach your goals.

Front Office Rocks

For years, dentists have asked me to come to their offices and solve their staff issues. I wanted to help as many people as possible and knew there had to be a better way to help more offices at one time. I also knew the front office is the biggest concern dentists have in their practice, and no one-stop solution existed to help them improve this area. In 2013, I started Front Office Rocks with the idea that dentists aren't trained in the front office and don't know what to expect. Often, the employees don't know what to expect, either.

Front Office Rocks provides online training both for new

employees and to help the dentist's current employees become more competent and successful at their jobs.

How do I know these strategies work?

I use them in my office every day. In fact, it is likely that someone in my office is watching a Front Office Rocks video right now.

I have hundreds of stories I could share about how offices are using the training to successfully improve their team and their front office. One practice subscribed to Front Office Rocks, then emailed four weeks later to tell me they had doubled their production and collections in that one month alone.

In another office, one employee watched three videos on her first day. The same afternoon, she received a call from a shopper—somebody calling around to ask, "How much is a crown?" Normally, she would have given the price, and the patient would have moved on to call another office. But because she was trained to handle the question, she turned that shopper's call into a consultation. The patient came in that afternoon and closed on a crown.

The profit from that crown paid for a year's subscription to Front Office Rocks on the first day of training. I have more stories than I can count just like these.

In the same way Front Office Rocks is a great resource to train your front office, this book can become your resource to understand what you should expect from your team and how to successfully step away from the drill to manage your dental business.

What to Expect

This book is not a training manual.

It is impossible to give you an exact solution, as that changes from office to office. If you're looking for something like that, Front Office Rocks can help you. It is continually updated and can be used to build a comprehensive employee handbook with your preferred policies.

What this book *will* do, however, is help you understand what to expect from your team and how to know if those expectations are being met. You will learn what your purpose is as the owner, what to expect from your front office staff, and how to communicate more effectively. You'll see what it takes to be a great captain, and you'll know how to run a tight ship.

I've organized the chapters based on five main areas of the front office. I suggest that you read this book from front to back and then share it with your team. Each section discusses the purpose of a role, what you should know about it, what you should expect your team to know, and how to hold your team members accountable.

I suggest you try not to rush through one section just to get to the next. However, if you have a certain pain point you are experiencing right now, you can jump to that section in this book to address it.

This is more than a how-to session. This book will change the way you lead your front office.

Speak the Same Language

You need to know how to manage your team, but that doesn't mean you need to know how to do your team's job. Your staff members know what to do. You need to learn how to help them to do it even better. Know your own expectations and how to hold them accountable.

Once you implement the right systems and training, you and your team will speak the same language. You will be able to sit down and have intelligent conversations with your team members about things you may never have learned but now fully understand.

Finally, you'll be able to go home on Friday nights and leave work where it belongs—at the office. Vacations will be within your reach. You can leave the practice without worrying about what will happen while you're gone. Contributions to your child's education costs and your retirement plan will be a reality, not a dream. And you can start enjoying dentistry again!

You can choose to create the practice you want.

It all starts with the right mindset.

Chapter 1

THE MINDSET

Have It Your Way

Going to the dentist is not like ordering off the menu at a restaurant.

I went to Burger King for lunch the other day. I pulled up to the drive-thru and ordered. "Hi, I'll have a Whopper Junior with cheese, extra pickles, no tomatoes, with onion rings and a diet Coke. Thanks!"

I knew I could "have it my way."

After lunch, I went into a friend's office and overheard the dentist tell a patient, "You need two crowns, three fillings, and a night guard." The patient nodded in agreement to the treatment plan.

Then, she went to the front desk.

Even though the dentist had told the patient exactly what she needed, when she found out that her insurance wouldn't cover everything, the patient started picking apart the treatment plan like she was at a drive-thru. "Well, I'll do one of the crowns. I guess all three fillings, but I won't do the night guard."

Should we let her have it her way?

Not if we want her to get healthy. And not if we want the dental office to thrive.

The Business Hat

You already know how to be a dentist.

You wear your dental hat for the clinical aspect. You are comfortable in the operatory with the patient. You have the ins and outs of the delivery part of dentistry. That is what you were taught in dental school, and that is where you are most comfortable.

Now you have to step away from the drill and put on your business hat.

Your business hat covers everything that is not being a dentist. You have to know how to hire, fire, train, manage, and motivate your employees, in addition to so many other things that you were not taught in dental school.

You have to hire the right employees and get them the right training. Those employees have to answer the phones the right way. They need to know how to not only schedule patients for dentistry and hygiene, but also get the patients to actually show up for appointments. Your employees need to be able to talk to patients about their treatment, insurance, and money. Then, your team must be able to ask for reviews and referrals from other people.

You're in more than just the tooth industry. You are also in the people industry.

You don't get to work on many teeth if patients don't show up or if they cancel appointments. There is not a lot of dentistry going on if patients don't understand why they need certain treatments.

To fix this, you need to be not only a dentist, but also a business owner. When you know what to expect from your staff and from your office, you can serve up the best possible care for your patients. But where do you begin?

In order to wear your business hat effectively, you have to understand why you put it on in the first place.

The Why

You know why you perform dentistry. So why do you need to wear a business hat?

All of the systems, policies, and procedures are in place for the ultimate outcome of helping patients. If you tell your team to make confirmation calls or fill your schedule, those are just tasks. Your employees will be more successful if they also understand the purpose behind their actions. They need to know that the goal of everything you do is to help patients with their dentistry and dental health.

The way to help patients is to understand what you do, as

a dentist, but to also understand from their perspective what they *think* you do.

As a dentist, you offer a service that helps your patients live a longer, healthier life. In your patients' minds, however, what you do is stick drills and needles in their mouths, when half the time their teeth did not hurt before you started working on them, and then you charge them thousands of dollars for all of this.

Your customers don't actually want what you sell.

But they do *need* your services. Here is where the big "why" comes in. Nobody else looks out for your patients' oral health but you and your team. We are in a health-care industry, but we can't help people live longer unless they actually come in.

Everyone in your office needs to understand the business of dentistry in order to get patients in the office. Why? So that you can take care of their health.

Change Your Mindset

You and your team need to recognize that you are not selling anything fun.

If you give your patients options, they are always going to pick the cheapest one with the least amount of dentistry. You and your team need to follow through and make sure your patients arrive. You can't take it personally when patients don't want to get their dentistry done.

You and your team have to put the patients' needs ahead of their wants.

When people buy something, they don't typically just pick it up off the shelf and buy it. They think about it. They ask, "Do I really need it? Is this something I could spend money on now, or should I wait?" If your patient has to decide between a root canal and a big-screen TV, he or she isn't going to choose the root canal. The biggest mindset change you have to make is to understand that people don't want dentistry, but they need it.

That mindset shift starts with you, the doctor, and filters down through your team so that everyone works together for the best interest of your patients.

Customer Service

Your patients and prospective patients expect more from you than just quality dentistry.

Before new patients get to experience your dentistry, they make a decision about your office. They decide whether they like it based on how your phones are answered or how easy it was to get an appointment. Your new patients' impression of you has everything to do with customer service.

Patients judge you on so many aspects of your practice other than your dentistry. People look on the internet for reviews before going to a new practice. The reviews are not about the dentistry, but about the patient's experience in the rest of your office.

Regardless of how much marketing you do, your real reputation rests on customer service.

And that starts with you.

The Leadership Role

In your office, you are not only the dentist; you are also the leader.

Your staff needs someone to give direction, make decisions, and be the executive of the organization. A leader motivates the team. A leader makes decisions that are best for the office. A leader handles things as they come up, sets goals, and gets the resources needed for the team to reach those goals.

In order to change the way you lead your dental business, you must become a more effective communicator.

Your team needs to know the goals you are all working to achieve. To be an effective leader, you must have regular meetings with your staff so everybody in your office is on the same page.

Do you have expectations of your patients as well?

When you go to a restaurant, you see the sign that says, "We reserve the right to refuse service to anyone." As the leader of a dental practice, you have the same rights. You have to recognize what is best for your business. If a patient causes problems and gives you grief, that person can go somewhere else. You want to have the best team, the best policies, and the best patients.

Within your four walls, you have full control.

Through the Office

As an owner, you need to understand every aspect of your team and their duties.

You need to be an effective owner and manager. In order to do that, you should know what to expect out of your team in each area of expertise. But you also need to become more knowledgeable. You don't build a business only on people. You build it with knowledge and positions, and then you train the best people to do those jobs well.

It is important to understand each role and its pieces so you have a grasp of how it all comes together to achieve your goals.

The chapters in this book will give you that knowledge.

Each chapter provides information about a specific area or role in your front office, along with suggestions for improvements and specific things to look for. From purpose to accountability, and through the five major roles, you will learn successful strategies that work in any dental office.

Purpose. Purpose is the reason you get up every day and want to help your patients. You have to define your purpose and communicate it to your team members. Their purpose should align with yours.

Communication. Communication travels in two directions: speaking and listening. Effective communication in the dental office helps your patients understand why they need dentistry. You also need to communicate with your team members so they understand their roles and your expectations.

The Receptionist. The receptionist is the patients' first impression when they call your office. This is a vital position that represents you. I'll show you what to expect from a receptionist and the importance of the person who answers your phone.

The Scheduler. The scheduler ensures the schedule runs as efficiently and productively as possible. You will learn how this person can help you meet your goals and lower your stress on a daily basis.

The Treatment Coordinator. The treatment coordinator is anyone who helps you get the patient to accept treatment. This person needs to understand how to get patients through their questions and concerns, help them understand why they need treatment, and get them on board to complete the treatment.

The Financial Coordinator. The financial coordinator guarantees the patients have their financial arrangements worked out before the dentistry is complete and subsequently deals with the insurance companies. This position makes sure you get paid. You'll see why this role is key to ensure you have a well-run, profitable business.

The Office Manager. The office manager is the liaison between the doctor and the team. He or she helps you manage your team day to day. When you have a great office manager, you can wear your dental hat and still know that your business is being run the way you want it.

Accountability. Once you commit to doing things differently, you have to hold your team accountable to see things actually change. Change can be hard, and it needs to be managed. If you hold your team and yourself accountable, you can achieve the outcome you want.

When all of these pieces come together, the only limit on your office's transformation and success is your drive. If you implement the changes described here, your practice will begin to turn around. The initial changes can happen in a single day.

You will communicate better. You will understand the various roles of your front office team, and you will be comfortable wearing your business hat. You will see your business shifting toward your goals of greater control, fun, and profit within the first month.

The first step toward that destination is to set the vision for your office by discovering your purpose.

Chapter 2

THE PURPOSE

A Cautionary Tale

The most important part of running a business is knowing your purpose. But what happens if you miss this crucial step?

When my husband and I moved to San Diego, we sold our very successful, well-run dental office in Maryland to a dentist who wanted a second location. We worked closely with her for three months during the transition. We discussed how important it was to communicate with the staff and patients to make sure her purpose aligned with theirs. She needed to put on her business hat to successfully take over the systems we had put in place for our busy practice.

Unfortunately, this dentist couldn't take off her dental hat and put on her business hat.

She failed to define a purpose for that second office because she didn't see the importance of managing the business side of the practice. She assumed the employees would figure it all out for themselves.

Over the next three years, one by one, all twelve of the employees who had worked for us either quit or were fired. Patients fled. This dentist didn't connect with her patients or her team as the new owner of the practice. She didn't ensure the employees were in line with her goals, and she didn't work toward patient retention.

She missed the opportunity for great success by simply failing to share her purpose.

Three years after buying the practice from us, she sold it—at a huge loss—to a dental corporation. Without knowing how to communicate her purpose, she was not capable of continuing our thriving business. She certainly missed her goal of owning a successful second dental office with a great team.

We're not going to let that happen to you.

Know Your Purpose

Your purpose is the reason you do what you do.

Ask yourself a few questions to find your purpose: What is your ultimate goal in changing the way you lead your dental office? Why do you do what you do? What outcome do you expect from your effort?

If you don't have clear answers to these questions, you may not understand the reason behind what you do daily. You simply perform your tasks and duties. But once you identify the intention behind your daily tasks, you will have greater control and see much better results.

When you understand your purpose, the desired result is clear. The outcome matters, so there is a higher level of success in achieving it. When you communicate it with your team members, they can work toward that goal with you. However, if you don't know your purpose, you cannot share it. Your team members won't see the bigger picture or their part in it, and they will just do the daily work without concern for the outcome or results. This leads to frustration and a group of people all going in different directions.

Because you are a dentist, your goal is to help patients. This chapter looks closely at your purposes, which vary depending on which hat you're wearing. You must align these varying purposes between you as the dentist and you as the business owner.

Multipurpose

Do you have a clear understanding of why your office does what it does? How do your purpose and visions differ between you and your team? And how do you get and keep them aligned?

Let's start with you.

The Dentist

The best way to identify your purpose as a dentist is to think about why you got into dentistry in the first place. What did you envision in your practice?

It's okay if you haven't arrived at the same place you once envisioned. Recognizing the disconnect helps determine where you are and where you want to go. Figure out why you chose dentistry, and that's your purpose.

Now, write it down; don't just think about it. This is an important step.

When you write out your purpose, your chances of achieving it are higher. Beyond solidifying it in your mind, it makes your purpose easier to share. When you share your purpose, you hold yourself accountable.

When you begin to feel yourself veer away from this clearly defined purpose, go back and revisit it.

It's easy to make excuses. It's easy to say that not every day is going to be in line with your purpose. But when it is in front of you, it is easier to compare your daily decisions against your goal.

The Business Owner

Your purpose as a dentist is most important to you, personally. But for this book specifically, we want to help get your front office systems and team in line, so the main focus is on your goal as a business owner.

As the owner and the doctor, you decide the purpose of your office. What did you plan to achieve when you became the owner of a dental business? Why did you make the leap from an associate? Why don't you work at the local health clinic?

Chances are you want to help patients with dental health, but you also want to make money and be your own boss. Knowing your purpose can help you achieve both your clinical and your business goals.

Write down your goals from a business perspective. Remind yourself why you decided to open your own practice. Determine where you are and where you want to be, and identify what is missing between the two.

Keep your business owner purpose alongside your dentist purpose. Once both of these are clear, you can share them with your team.

The Employees

For your employees to understand your purpose, you must communicate it.

Schedule a team meeting when everybody can step away from their patients and day-to-day duties. Get everybody together, at least on an annual basis, to discuss your purpose.

Your employees want to help you achieve your goals. But

if they are unsure of what your purpose is, they can't help you. During the meeting, describe your vision and discuss your goals. Agree as a team on what drives the office and what sets your practice apart from any other.

Once your staff members understand your vision for the office, make sure that their purpose aligns with yours.

Have each team member write down his or her purpose from his or her position's perspective. Ask, "Why did you take this job? Why do you get up every day and come to work and help patients?"

Then, have everyone share their purpose with the team.

Your team members may share something profound with each other. When that happens, it bonds you with your employees and the team members to one another. Remember to share your purpose anytime someone is added to the staff, and ask the new hire's purpose right away. Ensure that, throughout training, the new employee is getting both the "how-to" of his or her job and the "why" behind it.

During this process, you may discover that one team member is not motivated to achieve the same goals. Or worse, that person may actively work against you and your goals.

If any of your staff is not in line with your purpose, you must take off your dental hat and put on your business hat. To get in control of your practice and move it forward, you have to address this issue and possibly part ways with any employee who does not share or support your goals. I know this may be hard, but remember this is not family, but rather a person who gets paid to do a job for you. Your team will be stronger and your purpose more defined.

Once your employees are on board to help you achieve your goals, post your purpose in the office and keep your employees' purposes in front of them. Each month, share the statistics and your progress toward those goals.

And always support the team that supports you.

Try to acknowledge employees who do a good job working toward their purpose. You can recognize people in a staff meeting or mention it in your morning huddle. Give examples of how a team member handled something really well. Your team members will know you are paying attention and they matter to you. When they feel noticed and appreciated, they will give more than 100 percent back to you, back to the practice, and back to your goal.

You want employees who want to grow personally and professionally with your practice.

The Patients

You can share your purpose with your patients as well as with your team.

I am not suggesting you walk all of your patients into the break room to show them the team's purpose and each person's goals. Instead, repeat specific parts of your purpose during their care. And make your purpose clear in the way you present yourself, your team, and your office.

It's one thing to tell patients your purpose, but it's another thing to show it to them.

Let's assume your purpose is to help patients get stable and healthy by helping them get rid of all their cavities and gum disease. But when they come in, you diagnose only what their insurance covers and you leave broken teeth and active decay in their mouths. It doesn't matter what you say; you're not actually doing what you told them—and yourself—that you would do.

Live by your purpose.

You are here to help people. The more your patients and staff hear you say that and see you do it, the more people you will help. As a bonus, you are also going to get more referrals, have a happier staff, and grow your business.

Look in the Mirror

It's possible that you might not have found your purpose yet. If that's the case, maybe you just haven't looked in the mirror and said, "What can I do about this?"

It's a lot like losing weight.

We understand how to lose weight. We know that it's about eating right and working out. But we blame other things: there's not enough time, we're really busy, we travel a lot. So we don't make it to the gym. We don't eat healthy food. And we don't lose weight.

When we make excuses, nothing changes.

But when we look at ourselves and say, "What can I do? What do I want to achieve? What is my purpose behind all of this?" then we make progress.

Your dental office is no different.

Make excuses and nothing will change within your four walls. Or, you can recognize you play a part in where you are right now. It's not easy to take responsibility for that, but once you start, you will change the way you lead. Identifying your purpose can change the way your practice runs, the way you see yourself, and the growth of your practice.

It begins with looking in the mirror.

Once you define your purpose and know your staff's purposes are aligned with yours, you can all start moving in the same direction. To do that, you must be a leader. The next chapter will teach you the most important aspect of leadership: strong communication.

Chapter 3

COMMUNICATION

A Chat over Coffee

In our office, we have a huddle that starts at 7:30 each morning. One day, our dental assistant showed up to the huddle fifteen minutes late, carrying a coffee from Starbucks. "I'm sorry I'm late," she said. "Traffic was really bad."

What would happen if I did not talk to her about her showing up late? We would start the day frustrated she did not arrive on time. The others would see she arrived late and nothing was said. Some may even start to show up late themselves, assuming if it is fine for one, then they can all do it.

Instead, we addressed it immediately, while it was still a small issue.

As soon as the huddle ended, I asked her to step into my office. "You understand that the huddle starts at 7:30, right?" I asked.

"I understand," she replied.

I looked at the coffee in her hand. "I know you said you ran late because of traffic, but it looks like you stopped at Starbucks. Did you know you were running late?"

"I did," she said. "But I really needed my coffee."

"Okay," I replied. "But I need you to know that, as your employer, it's important to me that we start the huddle every day on time. It's difficult for the team to begin the day when everybody isn't here. What changes can you make to ensure you're here on time?"

"Well, maybe I can leave fifteen minutes earlier," she said. "Or I could have skipped Starbucks."

I nodded. "Great. So we have an understanding that you need to be here by 7:30?"

"Yes. I'll be here."

That scenario had to be handled by communicating with the employee swiftly and in the moment. By doing so, we prevented the situation from getting worse.

This level of communication needs to take place in your dental office, too.

Let's Talk

What is communication?

Communication is the imparting or exchanging of information, and it is a means of connection between people.

In a dental office, communication is constant and occurs among the staff in various scenarios throughout the day. This includes patient handoffs, scheduling, treatment planning, phone coverage, and conversations pertaining to patient care. In each scenario, communication is only as effective as both the speaker and the listener. You must be as effective a listener as you are a speaker in order to communicate any message.

It is vital you and your team have not only good communication, but the right kind of communication. Your day depends on it. When everyone is on the same page, the team is happier at the end of the day, and you are more likely to hit your profit goals. On the other hand, when you don't have effective communication, the day stagnates or gets chaotic. You are left pulling your hair and wondering what went wrong.

They didn't teach you about effective communication in dental school.

As the owner of a dental practice, you must step away from the drill and learn to communicate well. When you understand the importance of good communication, you can help your team implement it in your practice. This lowers the stress level in the office. Your team will understand your purpose, and the path to achieving your goals will be clear.

In this chapter, I discuss the key principles of communication and communicating as a leader. Let's start by looking at how to communicate clearly and effectively.

Six Key Principles of Effective Communication

Below are six key principles to help improve your communication. These principles are designed to make sure your team talks to you appropriately and you are clear with your employees.

Focus fully on the speaker. Communication is more than just the words we say. Nonverbal clues indicate if the person you're communicating with fully understands your message. Both the speaker and the listener can communicate by focusing on the other person. In this way, the listener receives the message and the speaker knows that he or she is being heard.

Avoid interrupting. This works together with being a good listener and focusing on the speaker. If you are thinking of the next thing you are going to say, you are not listening. When you interrupt, you cut off what the other person wants to say. This is disrespectful and poor customer service. Practice listening wholly to the other person and giving him or her respect.

Give the right amount of information. You need to know the right amount of communication. Giving too much information takes too long. It's not efficient, and it can be confusing. If a patient runs late, you don't need to know the full story behind it from your

employee. You need to know when he or she will be
there and if the delay will affect your schedule. On
the other hand, too little information can also lead to
confusion. If you tell a team member to set up a room,
that person needs to know what procedure to set up
and how long you'll need that room.

Avoid being judgmental. The purpose of communication is to express ideas. You have to respect the
person enough to value his or her thoughts and opin-
ions, whether you agree with the individual or not. If
you're judging someone, you are not fully listening.
This is important to discuss and practice with your
team. You all work in different areas, but you all want
to work together to solve issues within the practice.

Consider the right time and place. People who are
not trained in good communication tend to speak
when something comes into their head. You have to
consider whether it is the appropriate time for that
communication. For example, if something needs to
be handled right away, your staff should alert you,
verbally, at the time. If it's something you don't need
to know immediately, it can be written down and
shared later. You also have to consider if it is the right
place to share that message. Think about what should
be shared in front of patients and what should be

discussed privately. This will create the most efficient communication in your office.

Show your interest. You should be interested in what the other person is saying, and you want to show that interest. This is a big part of customer service and connecting with your employees. Don't multitask or look away; instead, be respectful as a listener. People like to know that others are interested in them. When you listen to people, it shows that you value them as patients in your practice or employees on your team. Teach your team to show an interest in your patients and what they have to say.

These principles span both verbal and nonverbal communication.

What you say is only a small part of communication. How you say it and your nonverbal cues also play a significant role. You can say one thing but give nonverbal responses that mean something else. For example, if you agree to do something but then cross your arms and roll your eyes, your action sends a different message than your words do.

Feedback can also be nonverbal. Looking at the speaker shows you are receptive to the message. Tracking him or her signals you are engaged. Nodding your head indicates you understand the message. All of these nonverbal actions communicate your interest in the conversation.

Nonverbal communication is especially important because, if you don't manage it well between your employees, it can lead to gossip and drama.

Less Gossip and Drama

Gossip and drama are prevalent in dental offices. Nine out of ten offices have experienced this damaging problem.

If you don't nip it in the bud each time it rears its ugly head, it will fester in your practice. Effective communication can stop gossip and drama before it takes root.

Gossip and drama start small, usually with one person concerned more about what someone else is doing rather than what he or she needs to do. Often, a problem begins with a misunderstanding. Perhaps someone was talking and the other person acted dismissively. Or, responded shortly. Or, didn't give feedback and didn't know what the speaker meant by what was said. There was a breakdown in communication somewhere.

Not everyone communicates the same way.

Some people are more sensitive than others. Some are more direct. You have a team built of different people with different personalities, and they each have different styles of communication. Take the time to learn more about your team's personality types to better understand how to communicate with them. Make sure miscommunication doesn't fester in the practice. Model good communication yourself.

Give guidance for fixing this issue, and make it clear that you don't allow gossip and drama in your practice.

Your purpose is to offer your patients the best dental care you can. Gossip and drama have no place in your practice.

Communicate as a Leader

To be a good leader, you have to hold yourself accountable for great communication.

A good leader leads by example. You must recognize that you may be part of the issue. Often, clinicians don't provide enough information. Your team may be the opposite and give too much information. Show your team members that you are trying to improve and motivate them to do better with their own changes. Respect is earned by joining them in the trenches and working hard.

Once you have shown your team members how to improve communication, hold them accountable.

Redirect with a quick comment. If you are with a patient and a team member starts to tell you something that is going to happen in three weeks, ask the person to write it down. This serves as a reminder of the right time and place for that type of communication. As you and your team redirect each other, your communication will flow better.

More Handoffs

A handoff occurs when a patient goes from one area of the practice to another.

One team member hands the patient off to the next. In the process, team members also hand off the communication about that patient.

During the handoff, your staff has to control the communication to include the right amount of information about what has happened so far during the appointment. It should be concise, and the listener should acknowledge the message. The scheduler has to communicate about the next appointment. The team has to address any questions or issues the patient has. Everyone involved must complete his or her part of the chain of communication.

Once you understand the importance of communication and how to work with your team to communicate well, your attention needs to shift to patient flow—the handoffs. The next chapters will discuss each of the five main areas of the front office, starting with the very first handoff: the receptionist.

Chapter 4

THE RECEPTIONIST

The Most Important Piece of Technology

Every dental office needs new patients. If you knew exactly how your receptionist was handling your phone calls, you might be astonished.

I often perform mystery calls to dental offices to hear how the receptionist answers the phone and responds to certain questions. Once, I called an office posing as a new patient and asked if they took my insurance. The receptionist said, "No, I'm sorry, we don't." So I asked for recommendations of dentists who did. And she replied, "You'll probably just have to call around. There are a lot of dentists who take that insurance." Just like that, she turned a new patient away.

During another mystery call, I called an office that didn't answer its phone at lunch. I left a voicemail and said I was new to the area. I mentioned that my family of four had just moved here, and I wanted to find out what it would cost for us all to come in as new patients. Before I hung up, I added that my husband needed a crown. I left my name and number and asked for more information.

I left that message four years ago . . . they still haven't called me back.

Another dentist asked me if it was really that important to answer the phone all the time. When I replied that it was, the dentist asked someone to stay during lunch and answer the phone instead of putting it on voicemail.

During that hour, they had seven phone calls. Two were new patients and five were existing patients calling to pay a bill or schedule an appointment. If someone hadn't been there to answer those calls, those payments would have been delayed, new patients might have hung up and called another office, and no one could have scheduled those appointments.

What is the common element of these stories? The receptionist!

What is the most important piece of technology in your office? Your CEREC or intraoral camera, perhaps? I agree that these are important and expensive, but I would challenge you that the most important device is actually the telephone. If the phones are not being answered correctly (or at all!), you are not going to have many patients who need your high-tech dentistry.

The Receptionist

One of the most important roles in your office is the receptionist.

The receptionist is the very first person patients talk to when they call your office. He or she is their first impression. As such, your receptionist must understand his or her importance in this role.

You want new patients, and you want to keep your existing patients. You want it to be easy for patients to speak to your office and to get in for an appointment. A good receptionist makes all this happen. If that first impression isn't handled correctly, you may lose current patients, and you certainly won't schedule new ones. The receptionist has the highest value when it comes to converting potential new patients into patients.

Many dental offices choose to start the newest people in the practice in the receptionist position. This is a mistake. You don't want the person with the least amount of training to answer your phones. You want to know that your receptionist is trained and ready to handle this responsibility and control the patient interaction.

The receptionist is the connection between your dental team behind the drills and all potential patients outside the office. If this employee doesn't do a phenomenal job, he or she will singlehandedly stop your practice from growing and profiting.

It is important to recognize that each dental office is a different size and has a different number of employees. Your office may have one dedicated receptionist, or you may have a smaller office where one employee wears multiple hats and "receptionist" is just one of many titles.

The hat of a receptionist is very different from the hat of an insurance coordinator, for example. A receptionist is happy and helpful and should give the caller his or her full attention, but an insurance coordinator is more detail oriented and focused on money and getting paid. It is important to note the difference so that no matter what position the person holds in the office, as soon as that phone rings, he or she puts on his or her welcoming and accommodating receptionist hat.

This chapter breaks down the role of the receptionist into four areas: reception-area organization and management, customer service and telephone skills, control of the patients in the reception area and on the schedule, and new patient phone calls and appointments.

Reception-Area Organization and Management

The receptionist is responsible for the overall feel of the reception area. He or she needs to pay special attention to its appearance and manage its environment.

Pay attention to the appearance of the reception area.
When a new patient comes into your business for the first
time, the first thing he or she sees is your reception area.

New patients haven't yet experienced your dentistry, so
they judge your entire office based on what they see around
them. The receptionist should make sure the reception area
looks clean, organized, and friendly. This means picking up
coffee cups left on the table, restocking the coffee area, putting magazines back after the patients have finished flipping
through them, and reducing clutter at the front desk.

When you go into the office tomorrow, take a look
around. Ask your receptionist to walk through it with you.
Does it need to be updated or cleaned? Can you fix any nicks,
paint the walls, or update the art? Small things make a big
difference—one that the patients will notice as soon as they
walk in.

Control the environment of the reception area. Patients
don't look forward to coming to the dental office, so you want
to make the experience as pleasant as possible.

Recently, I was in an office that had a TV in the reception
area. An afternoon talk show was on, and it was all about
sex. The news came on after that. It showed a terrorist attack
in another city and discussed how bad the economy was.
We don't want patients to get upset or be in a bad mood
before going to the back. Personally, I am against TV in the

reception area. If you do have one, make sure to manage the images that are shown.

You can choose to play pleasant music on a sound system in your reception area. Offer lighthearted magazines or something to entertain and distract the patients. The receptionist should make sure that the environment in your reception area is as friendly and comfortable as possible. This allows the patients to feel less worried and more secure and know you are there to take care of them.

What to Watch

- Does the receptionist clean up regularly?

- Does the receptionist restock as needed?

- Does the receptionist start and finish each day organized?

Customer Service and Telephone Skills

Another key aspect to focus on in this role is the people in front of the receptionist. Specifically, your receptionist should provide great customer service and build strong telephone skills.

Provide great customer service. The receptionist has to handle everything and everyone with exceptional customer service at all times.

Your receptionist should stand up when someone walks in, shake the patient's hand, and introduce him- or herself. Most importantly, the receptionist has to smile. Even if he or she is dealing with a ton of things at once, it is important to always try to smile and acknowledge each person with a welcoming, friendly, and inviting attitude.

The receptionist has to be able to handle anything that comes his or her way with good control and troubleshooting skills. Customer service—putting the patient first—is paramount to maintaining your current patients and gaining new ones.

Build strong telephone skills. Telephone skills are an important part of customer service. Remember, the telephone is the most important piece of equipment in the dental office.

Each time a receptionist answers the phone, he or she should smile and introduce him- or herself. Patients want to know with whom they are speaking. Your receptionist should use the patient's name throughout the conversation and use proper English without sounding too laid back. The phone calls should be appropriate and treat the patient with respect.

The phone should be answered by the third ring, and it should be answered all the time. If the phone rings longer or goes to voicemail, the patients get the impression that your office is too busy for them. They don't feel that you value them or their business. Your receptionist should not put people on hold for too long. If necessary, he or she can take a message and call the patient back.

Every person who calls your office should feel important to you and your team.

What to Watch

- Does the receptionist have solid troubleshooting skills?

- Is the receptionist friendly? Does he or she smile naturally?

- Listen to your receptionist. Do you like what you hear? Do patients say he or she is nice on the phones, or have you received complaints of rudeness?

- Listen to how long the phones ring. Are they answered by the third ring? Are they answered all the time?

Control of the Patients in the Reception Area and on the Schedule

The receptionist has a responsibility when it comes to getting the patient into the chair for his or her dentistry on time.

This means that your receptionist needs to control both the schedule and the reception area.

Control the schedule. The receptionist runs the schedule from the first minute patients arrive.

Your receptionist makes sure that paperwork is completed. He or she oversees the signing of consent forms, makes sure the patients update their medical histories, and makes it clear to the patients when the hygienist will be ready. If clients call to say they're running late, the receptionist has to determine how far away they are and if the office will still be able to see them.

The receptionist also helps the schedule run on time. This is determined by how well he or she communicates with the patients in the reception area.

Control the reception area. The receptionist handles questions and concerns from the patients. He or she needs to know what to do in different scenarios.

The receptionist needs to be able to help the patients get what they need while also doing what works best for the office and the schedule. He or she also works with patients who arrive early or who have to wait longer than expected. The receptionist stays in communication with the patients and gives them updates. He or she offers good customer service and makes sure the patients feel cared for while they wait.

The receptionist also must be aware of privacy and HIPAA

laws. For example, your receptionist cannot have a conversation with patients about a disease they have when there are other patients in the reception area. He or she has to be aware of all of these issues while helping the patients.

A good receptionist directs patients where they need to be so you can give them the best care possible in the dental office.

What to Watch

- Does the receptionist talk with the patients, communicating with them and making sure they are comfortable?

- Does the receptionist do whatever possible to get the patient in the chair on time?

- Does the receptionist ensure patient privacy in the reception area?

New Patient Phone Calls and Appointments

If your receptionist is doing a great job in the previous areas, he or she is ready for new patient phone calls. New patient calls should be treated with high priority, and the receptionist should be able to control new patient appointments.

Treat new patient phone calls with priority. New patient phone calls are the highest priority because new patients are the lifeblood of a practice. The receptionist must understand the purpose of these calls and how to handle them.

New patients don't know what to ask when they call a new office. The receptionist should find out more about the person on the other end of the phone. Why is the patient calling? Is he or she new to the area? Does this individual have a toothache, want a cleaning, or need something specific? That person is important, and the receptionist has an opportunity to bring him or her into your office.

Remember that you can't really sell the patient over the phone. You have to get the person into the office, where he or she will love you and your supportive team.

Control new patient appointments. The receptionist is the liaison between a nervous new patient and the unfamiliar dental office.

The patient will find every excuse not to show up, so the receptionist needs to understand how important his or her role is in helping that patient arrive. The patient and receptionist formed a connection over the phone, and that has to carry over into the first appointment. Your receptionist should take notes for the patient chart during the phone call, so he or she has something to discuss when the patient gets to the office.

When new patients arrive, the receptionist should greet them, welcome them, and show them the coffee area and restroom. He or she can help them complete their new patient paperwork if it's not finished already. Everyone should receive the highest level of customer service, but new patients should be treated like VIPs on their first visit. That sets the standard for the entire experience that a patient has in your office.

What to Watch

- How many new patient calls do you receive?

- How many of those new patients schedule appointments?

- How many of those new patients show up for their appointments?

Thank You for Calling

I made a mystery call once that highlighted the attributes of a good receptionist.

When I called into the office, the receptionist answered before the third ring. She sounded really pleasant and introduced herself before asking how she could help. I asked what insurance that office took. She replied, "We work with most insurances. Let me find out a little bit more about you before I handle that insurance question."

She then spent seven minutes on the phone asking questions about me and answering any questions I had with positive answers and genuine interest. I almost felt bad for not scheduling an appointment right then and there!

Now you have an idea of what a good receptionist does and why controlling who is placed in this role is so important. Who is next in the progression of handoffs?

The next handoff is to your scheduler.

Chapter 5

THE SCHEDULER

A Tale of Two Schedulers

A good attitude is the biggest difference between a good scheduler and a bad one.

In my office, Jessica is the best scheduler I've ever had. She gets to know all our patients, so she knows if they live close by and can come in last minute. She knows which patients prefer afternoons and which need morning appointments. She doesn't give up until the schedule is as close to perfect as possible.

If there is a cancellation, Jessica gets on the phone and doesn't stop calling until she finds somebody to fill that appointment. She keeps track of the waiting list of patients who want to get in. If the schedule has issues, she looks at it as if it's a game and feels pride when she rebuilds it.

Alternatively, I had a scheduler working for me previously who sighed and slammed down the phone every time a patient canceled. She was frustrated by the change and worked very slowly to fill it. This scheduler didn't understand that cancellations are a natural part of scheduling, and refilling the schedule when it falls apart is just one of the games we can play at our position in the front office.

She looked at each cancellation as a failure instead of as a puzzle to solve.

A positive attitude is the key factor of success in a scheduler.

The Scheduler

The number one cause of stress in every dental office, every day, is the schedule.

If the schedule is not built and managed effectively, it can defeat you, your team, your culture, and your dynamics. But a perfectly running schedule means patients are properly scheduled, the team works as a single unit, and you hit a profit goal every day.

The schedule is the backbone of how your practice runs.

The scheduler is the person in charge of the schedule. He or she makes sure the schedule is set up efficiently and effectively, and then monitors it for any changes. Although multiple people can be trained to take action in the schedule, there should be only one scheduler. One person needs to be held accountable for the schedule and take full responsibility for its management.

The schedule runs perfectly only approximately once every 365 days or so, but a strong scheduler will make your everyday reality as close to that ideal day as possible. When you understand this position, you can really take control of your schedule—and your day.

This chapter breaks down the four main areas of the scheduler's role: scheduling basics and hitting goals, the doctor's schedule, the hygiene schedule, and confirmations and cancellations.

Scheduling Basics and Hitting Goals

The schedule can make or break your practice. You should know why you schedule certain things and what you want to achieve with your schedule. Specifically, know your goal, schedule appointments appropriately, have a daily huddle, and have patients book their next appointment before they leave.

Know your goal. You don't want your scheduler to just put patients into the schedule to keep you busy. You want this person to put together a schedule that helps you hit your office goals on a daily basis.

It's important for you as the owner to know your monthly goal. How much do you want to produce and collect at the end of the month? Take that number and divide it by the number of days you see patients. The result is your daily goal. This is something your whole team should know and strive to achieve. It is vital that your scheduler knows and can plan your schedule accordingly.

Schedule appointments for the appropriate lengths. When it comes to scheduling, do your best to make sure you are allotting the appropriate amount of time for each procedure. Many times, the schedule is built on unrealistic timeframes for procedures, which results in the office running behind. This causes stress on the staff and doctor and creates unhappy patients. Why do we do that to ourselves?

Your scheduler should know the actual length of an appointment. The scheduler should build a realistic schedule that takes into account all of the factors that affect an office on a regular basis. When your scheduler knows how to allot the appropriate amount of time for each appointment, you have a better chance of running on time.

Have a morning huddle every day. The morning huddle is not just to talk about what procedures you have on the schedule. This is time to talk about the whole game plan for the day.

Verify enough time has been allotted for certain procedures. Discuss any areas that might get bunched up or where you can fit emergencies into the schedule. Are you on track to hit your daily goal? If not, where can you potentially find more production?

The huddle gets everybody on the same page and sets the pace, energy, and attitude for the day. This will help you, your scheduler, and your whole team run a realistic and productive schedule throughout the day.

Have patients book their next appointment before they leave. Nobody should leave your office without his or her next appointment. When patients schedule in advance, you can begin to predict your upcoming schedule and potential office growth.

It is easier to remind people to show up for an appointment than it is to track them down six months later and try to get them to schedule. Make it a priority to book every patient's next appointment. This will impress upon your patients the importance of their dental health.

What to Watch

- Do you hit your daily goal regularly?
- Do you run on time or behind?
- Do your patients leave your office with their next appointments?

The Doctor's Schedule

Again, depending on the size of your office, you might have just one person scheduling, but it's important to discuss the doctor's and the hygiene schedule here separately, as they should be built in different ways. When scheduling the doctor, your scheduler should build a production-based schedule and understand the three types of appointments.

Build the schedule on production. The doctor's schedule should be built based on production. The schedule does not need back-to-back appointments. The most productive appointments should be put into the schedule first, and other appointments can be booked around those.

Typically, you want 70 to 75 percent of your daily production goal from the doctor's schedule. The remaining 25 to 30 percent comes from the hygiene schedule. If your daily goal is $5,000, the scheduler should build the doctor's schedule so that it produces $4,000 that day. This method will help you hit your daily and monthly goals.

The three types of appointments. Each doctor's appointment can fit into one of three categories: primary, secondary, and tertiary. Primary appointments are high-dollar value appointments, such as crowns, endo, or dentures. In my office, anything $1,000 or more is a primary appointment. Secondary appointments have a dollar value associated with them, but it's lower than primary. Tertiary appointments have no dollar value, such as adjustments or evaluations.

When the scheduler is building the schedule, he or she should book primary appointments first. By doing so, the scheduler will have plenty of options to offer the patients, the office will hit the daily goal regularly—as primary appointments will help achieve that—and the day will be less hectic. Once 75 percent of the doctor's daily goal is scheduled, secondary and tertiary appointments can fill the rest of the day.

As the doctor, you may not be busy the entire eight hours of the day. That's okay. As long as you hit your daily goals, it gives you time to do hygiene exams, follow up with specialists, check emails, and complete other daily tasks. You want to schedule your goal to production, not to keep yourself busy the entire time you are in the office.

What to Watch

- Do you schedule to goal?
- What are the dollar amounts you scheduled versus the dollar amounts you actually produced?

The Hygiene Schedule

The hygiene schedule is handled differently than the doctor's schedule. The hygienist is expected to be productive, hitting 25 to 30 percent of the goal. But here, you want to pay special attention to keeping a full schedule and getting the patients to prioritize hygiene.

Keep the schedule full. A productive hygiene schedule should be full for the entire day. The hygienist will hit the daily goal by having as many appointments filled as possible.

Hygiene appointments are approximately the same length of time and of similar dollar value. So any time there is any opening for hygiene, the scheduler should try to fill it. Typically, however, the hygiene schedule is the first to fall apart. Patients move or cancel their hygiene appointments more frequently than when they schedule with the doctor. The cancellation should be filled by trying the patients with the highest likelihood of taking that appointment.

Get the patients on the schedule. It is easier to get patients to schedule dentistry than it is to book their cleaning appointment. If they have a cavity or a toothache, it hurts. They want to come in and get it fixed, and they know the appointment is in the next couple of weeks.

Your scheduler should ask patients, "Is there a day or time that works better for you?" He or she shouldn't just offer any time they want to come in. By offering appointments that are a win-win for both the patient and you, your scheduler will help keep your hygiene schedule productive and full.

It is more difficult to try to schedule patients for an appointment six months in the future. They aren't sure what their schedule is then. They say they'll call. Then, time goes by and they don't. I had a patient call and say she wasn't sure why she was getting a reminder; she had just been in, in July. When I looked, she had been scheduled in July . . . eighteen months previously! Your scheduler has to be consistent and persistent because you care about your patients' dental health.

Prioritize hygiene. If you and your team prioritize the importance of hygiene, your patients will notice.

Let's say a new patient comes in who hasn't been to the dentist for five years. You complete several treatments on him and get him healthy. But you don't pre-book him for his six-month cleaning appointment. When do you think that patient thinks he needs to go to the dentist again?

Talk to your patients from the first appointment about the importance of coming every six months. Your office has to make hygiene and oral examinations a priority so the patient will make them a priority too.

What to Watch

- Each day, what percentage of patients pre-book their next appointment? Do they stay on the schedule?

- Does your scheduler work with the right attitude to fill openings in the schedule?

- Does your hygienist hit the daily hygiene goal?

Confirmations and Cancellations

Every dental office has cancellations—that is the reality of what we do. You are not alone.

However, your scheduler should be doing all he or she can to keep them at a minimum. Your scheduler can help patients stay in the schedule and arrive for their appointments on time. Then, you can help those patients achieve and keep their dental health. It all starts with confirmation.

Adapt confirmation calls to the patient. The purpose of a confirmation call is to get the patient to arrive. The purpose is not to just leave a message. Communication with patients needs to be customized in a way that meets that goal.

If you schedule my mom for six months from now and she writes it in her calendar, she will show up. You don't even need to call her. If you schedule my son, however, you have to email him and text him the day before, and he still needs a call the morning of the appointment. If you call him again and tell him to get in the car because his appointment is in twenty minutes, he just might make it.

Your scheduler should get to know the patients and adapt according to what is necessary to get each particular patient to arrive.

Cancellations happen. We work with people. Sometimes people have legitimate issues that arise in their schedules and they have to cancel their appointment.

Your scheduler should be clear on your cancellation policy. When a patient cancels at the last minute, the scheduler should remind him or her of the policy. He or she should use clear communication to get an agreement from the patient that it won't happen again and should note it in the chart.

Chronic cancelers or reschedulers may need to be told they can't reschedule again or they can call in on a day when they are available and your scheduler can see if there is an opening that day.

If your scheduler is lax about this, he or she is setting up a culture of patients who think it's okay to cancel. That's not the kind of practice you want to run. You want a practice where you respect the patient's time, and the patient understands that your time is just as valuable.

What to Watch

- How many appointments get confirmed?
- How many appointments cancel?
- How many appointments reschedule?

A Rock in the Machinery

A schedule that doesn't run well causes a lot of frustration.

I once worked in an office that had three types of appointments, of various lengths, for hygiene. The scheduler didn't know which patient was supposed to get what type of appointment. And the hygienists were upset because they never had enough time. The front office blamed the back office, and the back office pointed at the hygienist. The hygienist pointed at the doctor, and the doctor ran behind schedule. It was a mess.

When I spoke to the scheduler, she told me that she didn't know why they had three different lengths of appointments: "It's just the way the office has always done it." Famous last words.

She and I worked out that all the hygiene appointments should be the same length—60 minutes. That simple change made the schedule easier to work with and gave the hygienist and doctor plenty of time. Their hygiene production increased by 50 percent.

Now the hygienists are happy. The doctor is happy. When the doctors and hygienists are happy, everyone's happy.

Now you know how to control the schedule to keep your office happy and fun. But you're not through the office yet.

In the next chapter, I'm going to hand you off to the treatment coordinator.

Chapter 6

THE TREATMENT COORDINATOR

A Secure Crown, a Secure Patient

I owe my extraordinary patient loyalty to my staff.

I managed a treatment coordinator who kept patients coming back because of her ability to clearly explain treatment and work. Her name was Ellen.

One day at the office, the dentist diagnosed a crown replacement for a patient. However, the patient's insurance covered a crown replacement only once every five years—and it had been less than five years since his last crown.

Ellen could have told the patient to just go ahead with it and left it at that. His $3,000 bill wasn't her problem. Instead, she called the insurance company to verify exactly when the crown in question had been placed.

She found out that the last crown had been done four years, eleven months, and two weeks prior—only two weeks away from the replacement being fully covered.

Ellen and the dentist delayed the procedure for two weeks, and the patient received full insurance coverage. He was thrilled. It was a win-win for everyone. In the end, the patient saved money and walked away with a long-lasting crown replacement. And we secured a happy, loyal patient.

This is just one example of the impact that a great treatment coordinator can have on your business.

The Treatment Coordinator

Your treatment coordinator is the person who helps your patients understand the treatment they need.

The treatment coordinator handles details. He or she addresses any questions and concerns the patients have. The person wearing the treatment coordinator hat is crucial because he or she is the liaison between the doctor behind the drill and the patients in the chair. If the treatment coordinator doesn't help your patients accept the recommended dentistry, you won't be able to help your patients or grow the business. Nobody wins.

A great treatment coordinator, however, is invaluable because he or she can explain what the patient needs, in language the patient can understand. The more you can help the patients understand your treatment plans and address any questions they may have, the more you can help your patients get healthier and live longer lives.

In this chapter, we'll discuss the five areas of the treatment coordinator's role. These areas include treatment planning, consultations and patient acceptance, discussing money, discussing insurance, and handling unscheduled treatments.

Treatment Planning

Treatment planning presents what treatment the patient needs and not only helps the patient accept it, but also clearly lays out the plan for scheduling and payments. Be aware that you should not compromise your treatment plan or let insurance dictate treatment.

Don't compromise your treatment plan. The treatment plan starts with you, the doctor, looking in the patient's mouth. You know what the patient needs to be healthy.

Sometimes, however, you might feel like you diagnose too much, or you worry about telling the patient that insurance won't cover your treatment plan. Clinically, you might know that your patient needs three crowns. But maybe, out of fear of a reaction, you diagnose only one crown and put a "watch" on the other two.

You do your patients a disservice when you hold back from telling them fully what they need.

What are you watching? If it's a problem now, it will likely develop into a more harmful, expensive problem in the future. Your treatment coordinator can speak with the patients only about what you diagnose. When you diagnose all the treatment your patients need, the treatment coordinator can help them better understand the need for it. Then you, your staff, and the patients can work together to improve their dental health.

Don't let insurance dictate treatment plans. You create treatment plans to help patients get healthy. Whatever insurance coverage they get or how many benefits they have remaining this year does not change what they need clinically.

Many dentists and teams slip into an insurance pitfall and allow their patients to pick and choose items off a menu like they're at Burger King. If you recommend two crowns, three fillings, and a night guard, your patient shouldn't decide against part of that recommendation once your treatment coordinator explains that insurance won't cover everything.

Let's be honest. Insurance companies are not looking out for what is best for your patients. They are not there to help your patients save their teeth. But that's what you and your treatment coordinator are there for—helping maintain the health of your patients.

What to Watch

- Do you diagnose only what insurance covers?
- How many treatment plans are being presented based on what the patient needs, rather than just what the insurance will cover?

- How many treatment plans do you offer each patient? If you have multiple treatment plans for one patient, you're letting them pick and choose.

Consultations and Patient Acceptance

The purpose of consultation, or treatment plan presentation, is to help patients understand what they need and get them on board to get it done.

The treatment coordinator essentially sells the dentistry. It is important that the treatment coordinator effectively educates patients on the sale. Would you ever buy something that you didn't understand? Of course not. You want the patient to fully understand his or her diagnoses, and your treatment coordinator should be involved to help.

Consultations between you and your patient are vital if you want the patient to arrive for appointments. You should involve the treatment coordinator in the consultation, use a consultation room if you have one, and—whatever you do—do not present the treatment or financials standing at the front desk.

Involve the treatment coordinator in the consultation. Your treatment coordinator can better help the patient understand your treatment if he or she is involved in the conversation with you. This is usually your one chance to get the patient to fully understand what he or she needs.

The treatment coordinator should know what the treatment plan is and why it is prescribed. If the patient looks like he or she doesn't understand, the treatment coordinator should clarify any technical terms or transition the conversation into descriptions or visuals the patient understands. The treatment coordinator may also be aware of information the doctor doesn't have, especially regarding insurance or concerns of the patient. He or she can then help the patient address those questions immediately, while the doctor is still in the room.

Use a consultation room. You and your treatment coordinator should hold treatment plan conversations in your consultation room, if your office has one. This removes the patients from the clinical area (normally not their favorite place), allows them a chance to relax, and lets you fully focus on their needs.

If you don't have a consultation room or quiet office outside of the operatory to transform into one, then at least remove your gloves and mask and speak face to face with the patient. The more comfortable you make them, the more likely your patients are to fully communicate their concerns and fears.

Don't hold consultations at the front desk. If you take away only one thing from this book, this is the most important change I want you to make. Stop presenting the cost of the treatment at the front desk.

> If you take away only one thing from reading this book, let it be this never present the cost of treatment at the front desk.

It is unacceptable to communicate with patients about what they need, how much it costs, and what their insurance will cover where other people are within earshot. Your patients are not going to tell you any real concerns if other people are listening. They will be uncomfortable, unwilling to commit, and out the front door as soon as possible, without returning for necessary dentistry.

When you hold a consultation in private, your patients can be more relaxed and ask all of their questions, and you have a higher probability that they will accept the treatment plan you present to them.

What to Watch

- What changes, if any, are made to your treatment plans?
- What is the dollar amount presented compared with the dollar amount accepted?

- How many patients are telling you yes and then not making appointments for treatment?

Discussing Money

You and your treatment coordinator sell the dentistry. Discussing dentistry and talking about the price are two very different things. Many times, dentists can talk about what the patient needs, but when the patient asks, "How much?" the dentist is out of the room like the Road Runner.

There is a value in your treatment, and your dentistry is worth the price. When you are confident in what you charge, that comes across to the patient and raises your case acceptance. To be most effective, you want to discuss money before scheduling appointments, give payment options, and have a signed financial plan.

Discuss money before scheduling. Patients aren't really sold until they figure out the money. If patients are put in the schedule but don't know how they are going to pay, you are going to get a lot of last-minute cancellations and no-shows.

With your dental hat on, you know this is important for case acceptance. Switching to your business hat also shows that addressing money up front with patients sets up strong financial systems in your office.

Think about the last vacation you booked. When you determined what flight you wanted to take, what was the first piece of information they asked for before they booked your flight? Your credit card! And why did they do that? To ensure there was a seat waiting for you on the plane and you would arrive on time to be in your seat.

Your treatment coordinator should be able to talk about money in the consultation and find out how the patient plans to pay.

Offer payment options. Typically, dentists allow patients to pay by check, cash, or credit card. You also want to have third-party financing options, such as Care Credit or The Lending Club.

Remember, you are not a bank. You don't want your treatment coordinator to offer in-office financing. With third-party options, the patients who don't have the money can finance their treatment.

In my office, we say, "You can pay by cash, credit card, check, or we have third-party financing options. How would you like to take care of it?" Your treatment coordinator should be confident. He or she is not asking *if* the patient would like to pay for treatment, but *how*. Your coordinator knows it is important for the patient's health, and that comes across to the patient.

Have a signed financial agreement on file. Make sure that you have a signed treatment plan and financial arrangements with the patient.

Even when you have coordinated payment arrangements with patients, guess what? Patients forget to pay. But when you have patients sign an agreement during the consultation, it is a reminder for them and for your staff.

This signed agreement helps your patients work out their financials ahead of time. They can address any concerns before they are scheduled. And you know that they take the appointment seriously. With these steps in place, patients are more likely to show up, which allows you to give them the treatment they need.

What to Watch

- Does your treatment coordinator take good notes on how the patient plans to pay?

- Do you have signed financial arrangements from your patients?

Discussing Insurance

I have a mission in the dental industry: to help dental offices change the way they take care of patients. We are health-care providers, not insurance companies. You and your treatment coordinator can help me with this mission if you are insurance savvy but not insurance driven, and if you limit pre-authorizations.

Be insurance savvy, but not insurance driven. Insurance companies are not looking out for your patients' health. *You* are looking out for your patients' health.

Questions such as "Our patient needs some dental work; how much insurance does she have remaining this year?" or "We have a new patient scheduled today, great! What insurance does he have?" show that you are being driven more by insurance than by what is best for the patient.

The treatment coordinator needs to understand the patient's insurance, including how his or her plan works and what it covers. This knowledge helps the coordinator with patient acceptance of treatment plans. However, we don't want the treatment plan influenced or changed because of insurance.

Limit pre-authorizations. The treatment coordinator is responsible for understanding your patients' insurance policies in order to clearly discuss the details with your patients. This includes understanding that a pre-authorization or a predetermination is just another way of allowing insurance to dictate treatment.

If you read the fine print when it comes to pre-authorizations, you'll find that insurance companies actually say that this is not a guarantee of benefits. They say that nothing is guaranteed until you actually perform the service. If a pre-authorization or predetermination is denied, does that mean the patient no longer needs the correlating procedure? Absolutely not. The treatment coordinator needs to convey your *practice's* policy that the patient's health, not the patient's insurance coverage, is the priority.

What to Watch

- How many pre-authorizations or predeterminations are submitted?

- How many phased treatment plans do you encounter?

- If a pre-authorization comes back denied, do you tell the patient he or she doesn't need the treatment?

Unscheduled Treatments

Even after your treatment coordinator has effectively done everything he or she is expected to do up to this point, some patients will leave your office without committing to a treatment plan. I recommend trying to get patients to schedule treatments the day of the consultation. Case acceptance is always higher if you can schedule while the patient is in the office. However, for patients with unscheduled treatments, your treatment coordinator should make an agreement with the patients for following up and should maintain detailed notes.

Make an agreement about next steps. Your treatment coordinator and patient should agree on a date and time to follow up about any unscheduled treatment.

You spend a lot of time with your patients to show them how much you care about their dental health. You want your treatment coordinator's follow-up to be consistent with the patients' experience thus far. It is still important that they get scheduled and come in for treatment.

Include detailed notes. You and your treatment coordinator need to put detailed notes into your patients' charts, especially if they have unscheduled treatments.

You should include notes about issues the patient has, why the treatment needs to be done, questions about insurance, and the follow-up agreement. You and your treatment coordinator deal with hundreds of patients each week. You can't remember everything about patient conversations, but reviewing notes helps recall the discussion. If you have clear notes, your treatment coordinator can keep the conversation going until the patient finally makes the decision to get the dentistry done.

What to Watch

- What does your outstanding treatment report look like?

- Is your treatment coordinator putting in notes? Are they detailed enough?

- Does your treatment coordinator follow up with patients who don't make appointments?

Something to Chew On

Your treatment coordinator is almost as important as your patients' teeth.

As the doctor, you have great medical advice and information. Yet your patient can't swallow the information if it's not broken into more digestible pieces.

The treatment coordinator helps to do just that. Enable him or her to translate your information into layman's terms, so patients understand treatment plans clearly and can make their appointments. This is all going to quickly enable your practice to grow and become more profitable.

In the next chapter, we'll discuss a role that also supports your patients' understanding, but from the insurance side of things. It's time for the handoff to the financial coordinator.

Chapter 7

THE FINANCIAL COORDINATOR

Damage Control

Not many people like to talk about money. But a good financial coordinator can make that discussion much easier.

I have an amazing financial coordinator, Lisa, who helps patients understand that we look out for their best interests.

One of our patients of record, an insurance broker, referred a new patient to us and told him the insurance would cover it. The new patient came in and needed a crown. Despite what his friend had told him, it turned out that his insurance covered only a very small portion of the cost.

He was quite upset to learn that he had to shell out a pretty penny when he'd assumed he'd leave the office free of charge. He went online and left a terrible review about the entire scenario.

That was when Lisa, my financial coordinator, stepped in and talked him off the ledge.

Lisa explained we weren't in-network for his insurance, and the insurance broker had given him information without verifying it with us. She also acknowledged we had not discussed insurance much before the appointment. She took some of the responsibility for the problem, and she was understanding.

Because she took the time to see it from the patient's perspective, he had a calm discussion with her. She made him feel that he was listened to.

Ultimately, the patient understood that the insurance was the problem, not our office. And he respected the way we handled the issue. He took down the bad review and ended up canceling his insurance. Now he comes to us as a cash patient and has been a long-term client ever since.

It is not worth losing a good patient if you can somehow salvage the relationship. A good financial coordinator can help you do that.

The Financial Coordinator

Your financial coordinator ensures that you make a profit. You're in the business of helping people, working on teeth, and getting your patients healthy. But after all, it's a business, not a charity. If you're not getting paid, you're not going to be doing any of this for very long.

When filling your financial coordinator role, look for someone who doesn't feel awkward talking about money.

This person's job revolves heavily around his or her ability to discuss insurance with your patients, which can often be as enjoyable as a root canal. Still, it's important that your financial coordinator be capable of leading conversations in this department, because it frequently makes the difference between a satisfied patient and a disgruntled patient.

Your financial coordinator needs to understand the ins and outs of insurance, how to balance accounts, and how to talk to patients firmly, but with empathy. A successful financial coordinator will make sure you get paid in a timely manner. Your practice will see a low number of accounts receivable, which means you're most often paid for your work within thirty days of completing it.

With a good financial coordinator on your team, you won't be up at night wondering if you will make enough this month. You'll know your financial coordinator has it under control. Your office will run smoothly, allowing you to help as many patients as possible because you have the money to do so.

In this chapter, we'll discuss the five areas of focus for an efficient financial coordinator: understanding insurance, billing insurance and getting paid, balancing patient accounts, discussing balances with patients, and billing patients.

Understanding Insurance

As with the treatment coordinator, your financial coordinator needs to know the ins and outs of insurance. However, unlike the treatment coordinator, the financial coordinator needs to understand insurance on a more detailed level. He or she needs to help you be insurance savvy and be aware of insurance red flags.

Be insurance savvy. You don't want to be insurance driven, but your financial coordinator does need to be savvy about different insurance companies and their policies.

This person needs to have knowledge of in-network and out-of-network policies. If you're an in-network dentist for your patients, you charge them a lower fee.

The benefit for you to sign up with a particular plan is to bring in more patients. Essentially, you give the insurance-plan patients a discounted fee, and the insurance plans put you on a list of dental health-care providers. Now your practice is more visible and easily accessible. However, if you're an in-network dentist for a patient and your crown fee is $1,000, your associated insurance plan may allow you to charge only $700, for example. The difference is basically the cost to acquire that patient.

On the other hand, if your practice isn't contracted with a particular insurance policy or plan, you have more freedom to operate the way you wish. As we discussed, if you become too insurance driven, you sacrifice patient health.

Be aware of insurance red flags. There are a lot of loopholes in every insurance plan. In my office, we call them red flags.

Your financial coordinator should be aware of these red flags and disclaimers. For example, there may be waiting periods, missing tooth clauses, and downgrades. If he or she is aware of these ahead of time, your financial coordinator can make the information as clear as possible for the patient. The patient needs to understand that it is not great insurance. You and your staff will do everything you can to maximize the benefits, but you can't make an insurance plan better than it is.

What to Watch

- Does your financial coordinator understand insurance?

- Are there a lot of big balances on patients' accounts after insurance has paid?

Billing Insurance and Getting Paid

Following treatment, a good financial coordinator generates the insurance claim with all the appropriate treatment codes, narratives, and radiographs and submits it to the insurance companies in a timely manner. This is to make sure you get paid. I suggest that your financial coordinator submit complete claims within twenty-four hours of treatment, make sure you receive a response within thirty days, and follow up on outstanding claims.

Submit complete claims within twenty-four hours of service. When you finish the treatment, you mark it as complete in your software. Then, the insurance claim can be generated.

Your financial coordinator should submit everything the insurance company needs along with the claim. Make sure to complete your procedure notes by the end of every day so that the claims can go out as soon as possible. I recommend electronically submitting claims within twenty-four hours of providing the associated service. The faster the claim goes out, the faster you'll receive payment.

Make sure you receive a response within thirty days. You should not submit paper claims. Everything should be done electronically, so that you get paid quickly and so you have a record that the claim has been received.

Once a claim is submitted, the clearing house ensures that you've included all relevant information (such as x-rays and radiographs) and sends it along to the insurance company for evaluation. In most cases, you should hear back from the insurance company within thirty days. If you do not, your financial coordinator is responsible for the follow-up with the insurance company to see the process through.

Having an efficient financial coordinator means that you don't have to deal with insurance companies and you still get paid on time.

Follow up on claims. Every plan has a certain period of time during which you can submit the claim before it's too late. If your financial coordinator doesn't follow up, the insurance company might delay until it no longer has to pay.

There are times when the insurance does pay, but it doesn't pay what it should. A good financial coordinator will recognize that and bring it to your attention to decide whether or not it's worth fighting the insurance company. Sometimes, with a little persistence and more information, the insurance company will reevaluate and pay a higher amount.

It pays to have a financial coordinator who is detail oriented and organized. Dealing with insurance companies is not necessarily the most enjoyable part of the job, but it is the part that helps you make money each day.

What to Watch

- How many outstanding claim reports do you have?
- How many are at thirty, sixty, and ninety days?

Balancing Patient Accounts

Balancing patient accounts is the most significant part of the financial coordinator role. This is where you have the most potential for unhappy patients. A good financial coordinator will know where a patient's balance comes from and underestimate insurance payments rather than overestimate.

Know where the patient's balance comes from. At the time of the treatment plan acceptance, you reviewed the impending procedures with your patient and what these procedures cost. You estimated what insurance would cover. Perhaps the insurance was set to cover everything. Now, your patient has received a bill and has a balance on his or her account.

If your financial coordinator can't explain where this balance originated, you will have a disgruntled patient.

I stress the importance of this so much because in most cases, this is why patients are turning to the internet and giving your practice a poor review. "The dentist's office told me my insurance was going to pay X, but my insurance paid Y," they'll complain. "And now I have a balance!"

Sure, you prepared them for this when you discussed the treatment plan, but they won't likely remember that conversation. Now, your financial coordinator needs to look at the notes and signed financial agreement. He or she can remind the patients that this is really a problem they have with the insurance company. You can't help what the insurance covers; you can only estimate it.

Underestimate insurance payments rather than over-estimate. No matter how much your financial coordinator reminds patients that insurance is just an estimate, they are going to be unhappy if there's a balance on the back end. If you think the insurance is going to downgrade for any reason, underestimate the insurance payment.

It is better to underestimate what you expect the insurance companies to pay than to overestimate. If you overestimate, your patient ends up with a balance due and a bad feeling. But if your financial coordinator's estimate for the cost to the patient is slightly high, the patient can plan for the payment ahead of time and will be happy to receive a refund or credit in the end.

These are some things for your financial coordinator to be aware of in his or her conversations with your patients to thoroughly prepare them for a potential account balance at the time of billing. This leaves less room for surprises and encourages timely payments.

What to Watch

- How high is your accounts receivable?
- How many patient complaints do you get? If your patients are complaining about their balances and

not paying them off in a timely manner, you're losing money on those treatments you already performed.

Discussing Balances with Patients

As I said, incorrectly estimating how much insurance will cover is the top reason why patients give negative reviews of a dental practice. It's important that you have a financial coordinator who is up to the task of attempting to prevent that unwanted feedback. Your financial coordinator can do this by calling to discuss a bill and reviewing balances ahead of time.

Call to discuss a bill. Some patients need a phone call if there is even the smallest balance on their account. Some patients end up with a balance that is larger than expected.

I suggest the financial coordinator call these patients before they receive the bill to explain there is a balance and why. If you wait until the patient receives the balance and calls you, they are going to be upset. Worse, if you wait to inform your patient and he or she receives the balance late on Friday, the patient is going to stew in that annoyance all weekend and potentially head straight to Yelp before ever getting an explanation from you.

Review balances ahead of time. You'll have more success talking to patients about a balance when they are in the office rather than if you have to track them down. Knowing who has a balance before their appointment allows you to schedule time for this discussion.

Your financial coordinator should review patient accounts for upcoming appointments. If there is a balance, he or she can review it before the appointment. Then, the financial coordinator will be very clear on what the balance is from, whether your office has sent statements between the patient's last visit and this one and if there is still outstanding insurance.

Don't add treatments to your patients' accounts if they have an outstanding balance, and don't take the patients by surprise. With this review in place, your financial coordinator can speak clearly with the patients about their balances and get those balances paid promptly.

What to Watch

- How much of your accounts receivable is over thirty, sixty, and ninety days?

- Does your financial coordinator call patients with a balance at least monthly?

Billing Patients

Your patient's balance typically comes after the insurance payment. This is the opportunity for the financial coordinator to figure out where the balance comes from so he or she can explain it to your patient. After that, your financial coordinator should send a bill right away and have a plan for large balances.

Send a bill right away. The Explanation of Benefits (EOB) explains what the insurance covered. The patient receives the EOB around the same time as your office does, so it's important for your financial coordinator to send a bill immediately after.

If you send the first statement too long after the EOB, patients have a higher chance of forgetting why they have a balance. Then, they will get your bill and call the office, upset. If, however, your office uses electronic statements to send a bill within twenty-four hours, it will be easier for everyone. The EOB will be fresh in the patients' minds, and they will be more likely to pay you on time. You can then follow up by sending monthly statements and calls to patients with an outstanding balance.

Have a plan for large balances. Sometimes patients end up with a very large balance. Make sure your financial coordinator has a plan to offer patients a way to take care of that balance.

Your financial coordinator should work with patients so that they can take care of the balance they have with one of the options you offer. Whatever financing options you offer on the front end can also be offered for big balances after the fact. This way, you don't get stuck acting like a bank, and your patients have options to pay you in full.

What to Watch

- Does your financial coordinator send out monthly statements?
- Are patients' balances being paid after they receive the call or statement?

In Their Shoes

When patients call in, upset and threatening to leave the practice, they are not themselves. People tend to be irrational about money, and they feel hurt, financially, because nobody likes to have a bill.

Your financial coordinator is your patient's pain killer. This person is soothing but not pitying and able to put him- or herself in the patient's shoes. Good financial coordinators say things like "I understand why you're upset. I get where you're coming from." They listen to your patients, let them get out what they have to say, and then firmly bring them down off the ledge.

When your patients know they have been heard, they can start listening again.

And now it's time for the handoff to the final important role. In the next chapter, we'll discuss the second-in-command of your office—the office manager—and explain how he or she helps you steer your dental ship.

Chapter 8

THE OFFICE MANAGER

Door Trouble

I once worked in a dental office that had a pretty unique front-desk setup. It had one long counter with two workstations, but instead of the stations working side by side, they were separated by a floor-to-ceiling door. The door just stood there in the middle of the space.

What on earth is the purpose of that door? I wondered when I visited that office.

It didn't take long to find out. The two employees who managed the front desk didn't work well together. Worse, the dentist didn't know how to control the staff or the office drama.

This dentist's solution to the feud was to build a door and have his employees work on either side of it so they did not have to see each other during the day.

The whole situation was crazy. It was bad enough that they'd let the environment get that uncomfortable in the first place. Worse, this randomly placed door in the office looked ridiculous to patients. The practice had a ton of turnover because the dentist didn't have an office manager to help manage the staff. He allowed the employees to focus more on disagreeing with each other than on doing their jobs.

Ultimately, the dentist fired both employees and had to start over with a fresh team.

With a great office manager on your team, pointless drama like this never has to happen to you.

The Office Manager

While you're in the back of the office, tending to fillings, root canals, or crowns, you need someone in the front office leading the staff. This is where your office manager comes in.

Your office manager puts on the business hat of your practice for you, so you can be behind the drill, wearing your dental hat.

He or she acts as the liaison between you and your staff, and you and your patients. Basically, the office manager looks at things in terms of the big picture and guides your practice toward achieving your end goals of greater control, fun, and profitability.

When you succeed at the dentistry and your office manager succeeds in handling the practice's business, you can spend your time building your business rather than building doors.

In this chapter, we'll discuss the five areas that the office manager focuses on: job duties, patient control, managing the staff, doctor expectations, and teambuilding.

Job Duties

The office manager does everything necessary to run the office smoothly. This person's important job duties include scheduling the staff, making sure they're in the office when they should be, and opening the office. Your office manager covers all your bases and is always aware of and managing the practice's goals.

Cover all your bases. The office manager should oversee all the marketing, social media, sales, and IT efforts that help move your practice forward.

Your office manager also fills in during those "man down" scenarios. If the receptionist needs to take a sick day, for example, the office manager needs to sit at the front desk and handle the calls. He or she keeps an eye on everything and makes sure you always have your bases covered.

Remain aware of the practice's goals. When the office manager effectively does his or her job in helping other employees do theirs, the practice grows. If the office manager finds there is a weak link within the business, it's his or her responsibility to correct the issue either by counseling the problem employee or by finding the broken system and fixing it. The office manager should look at the office from a high level to not just manage the operations but also regularly look at the entire flow of your practice. He or she makes sure everything you need to hit your goals is in place. When you have a good office manager, staff members show up on time, do their jobs well, and help your practice grow.

What to Watch

- Are all the bases covered in your practice?
- Do you hit daily and monthly goals?

Patient Control

Your office manager is responsible for patient control. To manage patients well, he or she needs to think proactively rather than reactively. For example, when the office manager comes in first thing in the morning, he or she needs to review the schedule and ask, "Can we execute this schedule as is? What are some issues we may have throughout the day or week? What do I need the staff to do to avoid or approach those issues?" To have great patient control, your office manager has to align the team, troubleshoot and put out fires, and manage the office with autonomy.

Align the team. Your practice is there to help patients live a long, healthy life. If the office manager thinks some employees may prevent you from achieving that goal, he or she needs to handle it. This means making sure that everyone on the staff has the same goal for your patients and your practice. Your office manager is responsible for training the other team members to help get them on the same page.

Troubleshoot and put out fires. If patients want a discount or are upset about their payment balance, they will likely ask to talk to the office manager about their problem. Your office manager has to be able to troubleshoot and put out fires. Like your patients, your staff also needs a person to go to who can handle six issues at a time and help keep everyone happy.

Manage with autonomy. Independence is important for your office manager. This person has a lot of responsibilities. He or she needs to be empowered to take care of them without routinely checking in with you. The role of office manager requires a high level of autonomy and problem-solving ability. If your office manager leans on you too much, it will disrupt the flow of the office.

What to Watch

- Is the schedule falling apart?

- Is the team running smoothly?

- Can your office manager make decisions without you?

Managing the Staff

When it comes to managing the staff, the office manager role can be a lonely one. Your office manager is not the owner and doesn't have full decision-making power. At the same time, he or she is also not just one of the team.

Sitting in this middle-man position can cause a problem for office managers if they're not careful. The office manager needs to strike a steady balance from this angle, so that the staff respects the office manager and isn't going directly to you, the dentist, with problems. To do this, the office manager needs to lead the team, hold routine staff meetings, and present a unified front with the dentist.

Lead the team. So that the office manager can find the right balance in the office dynamic, it's important that you help enforce the idea that the office manager is in charge. If your team members aren't getting the answer they want from the office manager, that doesn't mean they can come to the dentist for a second try.

Have the office manager's back when he or she tries to enforce authority.

Hold routine staff meetings. You and your team need to establish a high level of trust in the office manager. One thing your office manager can do to promote this is to hold regular meetings with the staff members so that they understand their concerns are heard and their questions are answered.

Present a unified front. When the office manager earns the team's respect, the team will feel confident going to him or her with the tough questions. Your unified front with the office manager also sets a tone of ease for the office, which eliminates any unnecessary drama that may otherwise arise when things aren't in line at the top. You're setting an example for your team members, they're following it, and the practice is growing.

What to Watch

- Do you hold regular staff meetings?
- Do you and your office manager present a unified front to the team?
- How does the office "feel"? Is the office manager maintaining a good culture in the practice?

Doctor Expectations

Because the office manager acts as your right-hand man or woman, it's important that you allow the role some authority and decision-making power. This means you need to get on the same page as your office manager through regular communication.

Communicate regularly. If you don't prioritize regular and clear communication with your office manager, he or she will have a difficult time helping you succeed. This is a return of what we discussed in chapter 3.

As the practice's owner, you should take time to discuss your expectations with the office manager. Establish what you're looking for in terms of growth and outline what specific duties you'd like your office manager to handle. If you find that he or she doesn't handle a scenario the way you'd hoped, take that opportunity to constructively critique the approach so that your office manager reaches your expectations going forward.

The more you communicate and set aside time to meet with your office manager, the more trust you can have in his or her performance. This is how you create a partnership that allows you to work as the dentist, while the office manager successfully handles your office operations.

What to Watch

- Do you hold regular meetings with the office manager?

- How many projects are implemented and completed?

Teambuilding

Employee motivation and excitement are key to your practice's success and growth. If your team isn't excited to work for you and looking for ways to work toward your goals, you're going to have a hard time achieving them. Your office manager supports teambuilding by motivating your employees and arranging team activities.

Motivate your employees. Teambuilding is an important way to maintain your staff's motivation and excitement. The office manager is responsible for finding ways to encourage your employees in their roles. When he or she focuses on this task, your employees feel appreciated and want to grow with your company. Then, when things go wrong, you have a strong team of employees ready to put in the extra effort to find a solution.

Teambuilding does not have to be a huge event to make a big difference for your team. Maybe you take the time to celebrate each month's birthdays with a cake. Maybe you buy everyone coffee before the Friday morning meeting. Or maybe Mondays are your craziest days and you want to cushion the blow by ordering in pizza for lunch.

Arrange team activities. Your office manager can also arrange team activities outside of the office on occasion. For example, you all participate in a fundraising walk or go out for a night of bowling. These types of activities allow your team members to enjoy each other away from the office and learn more about how to communicate with each other—improving the openness and the productivity of the environment when they're back in the office.

People want to support businesses that have a welcoming, friendly environment. If you regularly take time to appreciate your team members, they'll work better with each other and your patients. Your patients will enjoy their occasional trips to the dentist. Everybody wins.

What to Watch

- Are your staff members happy to come to work every day?

- When was the last time you did something to motivate or bond your team?

A Healthy Partnership

Treat your dentist–office manager relationship the same way you would any other partnership in your life. Together, you two are changing the way you lead your practice toward success. Yes, you each have completely different roles in this partnership, but you both have the same goals in mind. When you strike this tone, it will fill your office, setting your team up to thrive in a productive, respectful, and secure working environment.

With this strong office structure in place, we can now move on to the next chapter and discuss what it takes to maintain it all: accountability in the workplace.

Chapter 9

ACCOUNTABILITY

Spa Day

In our practice, we created a game that exercised our team's accountability muscles.

We split into two teams to compete: the hygiene team and the dentist team. Each team had a production goal to achieve by the end of each day, and when a team achieved its daily goal, everyone on the team won a lottery scratch-off ticket. Then, at the end of the month, the team that most consistently hit its goals would earn a day together at the spa.

These contests and incentives sparked some exciting competition. Everyone wanted to win, so everyone supported his or her teammates and worked together to earn those prizes.

At the end of one month, we'd experienced our best production and collections ever. By offering these incentives, our practice saw a $25,000 jump in only thirty days. Instead of just rewarding the winning team, we treated the entire practice. *Everyone* deserved a spa day at that point.

Now, a spa day for a practice that size—eleven people—cost us about $1,500. But given the team's incredible success, it didn't matter. The accountability was next level.

This is just one example of the results you can get when you set your team members up for success and hold them (and yourself) accountable for your mutual goals.

What Is Accountability?

Accountability is the force that keeps your business moving forward. Without regular check-ins on your progress, you don't have control, and you don't know whether you're moving toward success. If your business is not moving forward and growing, it is actually shrinking.

Accountability requires you, as the owner of the company, to change the way you lead your team and make sure your employees complete tasks the way they should. As the dentist, you've set expectations for how you'd like your office to run, and it's important that you regularly step away from the drill and verify whether your employees meet those expectations.

After all, what good are goals if you and your surrounding support system aren't sticking to them? In the case of your practice, you and your staff members are each other's support systems.

If you don't establish any follow-through with your expectations, your practice won't meet its goals, which will stop your business's growth. Maintenance is key. Yes, ask your team to complete specific tasks and make sure that you've communicated the value of those tasks, but don't stop there. Check in regularly to see that the team completes the tasks you assigned.

When you and your team understand a goal, agree to work toward it, and hold one another accountable for it, everyone reaps the benefits.

The five areas of accountability that we'll discuss in this chapter are getting agreement, being consistent, having an open door, setting SMART goals, and recognizing successes and celebrating wins.

Get Agreement

The first step in holding you and your team accountable is establishing mutual agreement about the importance of your goals. Get your team on board with your plan. Again, this goes back to our chapter on communication. As the company owner, you need to set expectations for your team members and instruct them on how to meet those expectations.

In fact, say your goal *is* better communication. You can't come in on Monday morning and say, "We're going to communicate better. Now do it!" Instead, you need to sit down with your team members and explain where your communication stands currently, where you'd like it to be, how they see it currently, what they would like to improve, and how you'd like you and your team to reach that goal.

Your team should agree with you on all these aspects and be ready to work with you toward improvement. Once that agreement is established, you're ready as a team to move forward to better communication.

Be Consistent

After everyone is in agreement about your goals, it's important to stay consistent in your expectations for improvement.

You can't come in on Monday hoping to improve communication, establish that as a goal with your team, and then come in on Tuesday with a new area you'd like to improve. Monday, Tuesday, and all the days that follow must focus on the specific goal or goals you and your team originally agreed to work toward at the start of this process.

Consistency plays an important part in showing your team members that you're somebody they can rely on. It gives your team members confidence that when you set a goal, you do whatever is necessary to achieve that goal. When you are consistent, you establish yourself as someone they can look up to.

Have an Open Door

Welcome your employees' questions or concerns. When your staff members come to you to discuss issues, it shows they feel comfortable enough to talk with you. Some people work well with change, but some people do not. As the practice's leader, you have to be willing to work with some people a little extra when it comes to keeping them on the right track.

Of course, you have to know the difference between a concerned or nervous employee and a regularly complaining employee. If you have somebody who continues to push back, says the new direction won't work, or interrupts you throughout the day to complain, he or she may be a red flag. Ask yourself, "Does this person need extra hand holding, or is this person potentially causing trouble for the success of the practice?"

You own the practice. If you and the rest of your team agree on certain changes, you can't allow one employee to hold you back. Hopefully, with plenty of open-door communication, you and this red flag employee can find a way to settle on common ground. However, if you can't, you may need to consider parting ways.

Set SMART Goals

SMART goals are specific, measurable, achievable, realistic, and timely. Setting SMART goals helps you outline your practice's priorities and keeps you from setting your team up for failure.

Let's break down SMART goals.

"Specific" means that your goal can't be "we hope to increase our numbers over the next few months." That is not very specific. What numbers—production? Collections? Number of new patients? Goals that you are trying to achieve need to spell out what you are trying to accomplish.

"Measurable" is something you can measure. How many patients is "more"? Are you saying double what you did this year, or are you saying five more patients? Instead, you might say, "We want to go from ten to twenty patients next month." That's specific and measurable. Now we know that we have ten patients now and want to have twenty patients next month.

"Achievable" means you're not trying to quickly go from ten to one hundred patients. You'll cause an upset with your team members by putting a goal in front of them that's too unrealistic or too large for them to achieve. However, the goal also can't be too easy to achieve. Then, there's no motivation behind it. It needs to be something your team members feel they can do, but also something that they're going to have to put effort into.

This brings us to "realistic." Whatever you want to achieve needs to be sensible and accurate. For example, you're not going to say, "We want twenty patients who need implants to walk in the door tomorrow." You don't know which patients are coming in or what they need.

Finally, the goal has to be "timely." If a project or task deadline is too far out or too short term, it's not going to work. You can't say, "We need to double our patients by tomorrow." That's improbable. There's nothing I can do today that's going to double our number of patients by tomorrow. Then again, you also can't say, "We want to go from ten patients to twenty patients in five years." That's so far out that, again, there's no motivation behind it. It has to be something that motivates so there is enough energy behind it to make it successful.

If you find that you and your team are regularly missing goals, you'll need to reassess your progress and discover the breakdown. Go back through your SMART benchmarks and clarify that your goal has all those qualities. Also, ask yourself the important questions. Does your team agree with the goal? Are you staying consistent with what you want from your team?

Recognize Successes and Celebrate Wins

Once your team does reach success, recognize that and celebrate it! Remember the importance of teambuilding. If you quickly brush past success after success, your staff won't feel appreciated and will lose motivation, stunting your practice's growth. Recognize that even a step toward your goal is a success.

To celebrate, do something as simple as taking time out of your schedule to enjoy a team dinner or buy everyone a gift card to go shopping.

When you recognize successes and celebrate wins, your team members will look forward to coming to work each day and be excited for the next challenge you present to them. They'll enjoy helping the practice achieve its goals. Sure, keep looking for ways to improve, but always remember to get excited when you *have* improved.

Make Things Happen

As the leader of your practice, you're responsible for making things happen. Manage your team with accountability, so you can successfully implement the systems you need in your practice. As long as you follow through, you'll get more systems in place with less stress, and your practice will grow to be more fun and profitable.

In the next chapter, we'll take a look at the possibilities that are open to you once your office has a strong foundation. It's time for the final handoff.

Chapter 10

THE NEXT HANDOFF

Night and Day

One of my best clients is a husband-and-wife team.

The husband is the dentist and the wife is a hygienist. When we first met a year ago, she hadn't told any of their patients that she was married to the dentist. She did not want them to think she was in the role of office manager because she was married to the doctor. So she saw patients during the day. And at night, after everybody left, she stayed late to do the office management tasks. She had great ideas, but she couldn't implement them. It was too much work, and it wasn't fun anymore. She was burnt out.

She was afraid to share her purpose.

She wanted to grow the practice. She wanted to help more patients on a bigger scale. She needed to be the office manager.

After training with Front Office Rocks, we sat down with the team and talked about purpose. We communicated the doctor's goal and the team's goal. During that meeting, we found out that the whole team wanted her to be the office manager. She'd been in the industry longer than anybody else. They trusted her and her knowledge. They respected her—and always had.

She stepped up. And the results have been amazing.

This practice has more than doubled in the year since that meeting. The wife practices hygiene part time and runs the office the rest of the time. As a whole, the team is much happier and wildly successful.

Everything changed for the better when her purpose was aligned with the ultimate goal of the office—growth.

The Bigger Picture

You, as a dentist, went to dental school to learn to help people.

The right team, the right leadership, and the right system can help you achieve that goal. When your employees are motivated, are trained, and have the right attitude, they can follow you as you change the way you lead and make a huge impact on the population.

The best dental employees I've ever seen believe that they help their doctors with a bigger purpose. That purpose is to save patients' lives.

If your team members are empowered, excited, trained well, and held accountable, they play a huge part in this purpose. They are the front line with patients. Your staff members hold your patients' hands. They talk to people every day. And your team helps your patients get their dentistry done.

At the end of the day, yes, you run a dental office. You have numbers and goals to meet.

But you show up each day because you want your patients to live a longer, healthier life. That's the big picture. When you stay focused on it, everyone thrives.

The Next Handoff

Where do you want to go from here?

Dentistry is the core of your business. As you step away from the drill to become a better owner and leader, you see your business improve, and you become less stressed and have more fun. Now your business is thriving, and the control you've established allows you to take different roads.

Maybe you want an office that pays the bills and makes good money, but you have to work only three or four days a week. You can do that! You have systems in place in the front office, so your office will run like a well-oiled machine. I know a doctor in Michigan who grosses more than a million dollars with only 40 percent overhead, and he's open only three days a week. He has four days every week to be at home with his family.

It's possible that you are more valuable as the owner of the practice than as a dentist. This is what my husband decided. He brought on associates, so he sees patients clinically only a day and half to two days a week. The rest of the time, he handles the systems, the management, the treatment presentations—the whole flow of the business.

If you don't want to be bent over patients every day for the next forty years, bring in great dentists. Build your business as an owner. Have an organization where you can come and go. When you're not tied to a single-practitioner practice, you can travel for weeks at a time! That freedom is yours, and the practice still runs smoothly.

Maybe you want to open a second practice. If your systems run well and your first practice is hugely successful, take what you've implemented in Location A and apply that to Location B. You will be able to buy another practice or start the second office yourself.

What are your interests? Where do you want your career to go?

Your dental practice is the foundation of whatever you want to build. It will allow you the opportunity to go forward with wherever your personal purpose takes you.

Build a Bridge

The moment you picked up this book, you took the first step toward running a successful dental office. And this is only the beginning.

You care about your team. You know how important your front office is. Now, you understand more about your front office team members, the hats they wear, your different systems, and how to manage them. You're ready to change the way you lead your practice by implementing all the technical systems you need to support your front office.

And yes, it will be a lot of work. But you don't have to do it alone.

Front Office Rocks

I'm here for you.

My website, Front Office Rocks, is designed to help doctors like you and your team. It is available online, twenty-four hours a day, seven days a week. I designed this website with you in mind. I want it to be the resource you turn to, to get all of this information and training woven into your practice. Reach out to me at any point. Share articles and policies with your team. Listen to and watch webinars. I am here to help you and your team stay motivated as you set goals and work to hit those goals.

Front Office Rocks is your go-to solution to help your team members with their day-to-day duties. There, your staff can learn the ins and outs of things like offering an appointment to a patient or how to fight the insurance company on a claim.

Front Office Rocks is a dynamic tool and is updated on a regular basis. This book is a reference guide for what you need to know about each area in your office, and that isn't going to change. But the dental industry itself is always changing.

Front Office Rocks is an ever-changing place to visit to always get the latest and greatest information to run your office at the highest possible level.

You took the first step. Now, you can keep moving in the right direction.

Teamwork Rocks, Too

Do you know who else is there for you? Your team.

Have your team read this book. It was written to you, the doctor, so that you can understand the front office. But sharing it can also help you communicate with your team members. It will allow them to garner a greater understanding of their jobs.

You have a support system with your team. You just have to step away from the drill to get on the same page—and you can find that page in this book.

Whether you ask your staff members to read the entire book or just the one or two chapters that really speak to them, you will tap into that support system. Your team members want to help you. They know they can make an impact on the practice. They just need the right tools.

Talk about what you've learned from this book. Communicate your goals for your team and systems and office culture. And you will all come together to help your patients.

Within Your Four Walls

My wish is for you to know how important you are to your patients.

I want you to recognize how much of an impact you make in your patients' lives. I want you to know that every little detail makes a difference. You help people live a less stressful, longer life—a *better* life.

We make such an impact on our patients' lives. Remember that. Let it drive you. You can make a huge impact within your four walls.

And when you do that, the whole world opens up.

INDEX

ABOUT THE AUTHOR

Laura Hatch is the founder and CEO of Front Office Rocks, the leader in on-demand front office training for dental practices. After twelve years as an office manager and building two from-scratch dental practices, she switched gears to teach other dental owners how to manage and empower their team members. As the leading authority on front-office training, Hatch helps dental professionals improve their practices through online video courses, live seminars, and coaching.

Hatch has authored more than two hundred articles for leading dental publications and websites such as *The Progressive Dentist*, *Dental Assisting Digest*, *Dentaltown*, and *Dentistry IQ*. She is a fellow of the American Association of Dental Office Managers as well as a national and international speaker for dental authorities such as AADOM, Patterson, and Mid-Atlantic Dental Society. Hatch was also recognized as one of Dental Products Report's Top 25 Women in Dentistry for 2016.

When Hatch isn't managing at the practice or looking for innovative ways to bring more expertise and value to Front Office Rocks, you can find her on Dentaltown or in her own

"Ask Laura" forum, where she responds to dental team members' questions and shares her experience and knowledge as a dental office manager. She lives in San Diego, California, with her husband, Tony, and their two children, Nick and Alex.

Transform Your Team

Transform Your Team and Perform to Your Highest Potential

Have you witnessed a "great divide" between front office staff and the clinical team? Back office wonders why the front doesn't schedule better, while front office wonders why the back doesn't work faster.

Similar to the power of a schedule to make — or break — a practice, a high functioning team is essential for success. An effective team relies on solid systems and continual training to ensure performance and profitability.

This high energy, interactive course focuses on the skills and protocols needed to implement effective systems, enhance communication, and build a high functioning, cohesive team. As founder of Front Office Rocks online training and a dental office manager herself, Laura Hatch brings to life key concepts for empowering team members to improve performance and keep their focus on the principals of a successful practice. We'll focus on every process where team members impact patient perception of their experience. This course also focuses on how to deal with one of the biggest issues in the dental office: cancellations and no-shows. Learn how to get your patients to appoint, pay, and show up for their appointments!

Course Objectives:

- Learn techniques for turning conflict to cooperation
- Stop the cycle of complaints and gossip and increase employee productivity
- Identify time management issues and solutions
- Understand how to set and achieve production goals
- Develop exceptional patient and interoffice communication skills
- Learn how to design the schedule for ultimate productivity

Format: Full or Partial Day; Lecture, Workshop
Audience: Dentist and Team

FRONT OFFICE *Rocks*

ROCK STAR FRONT OFFICE TRAINING

Made in the USA
Monee, IL
06 October 2023

44088366R00079